BOOK ANALYSIS

Written by Alba Díez de Ure

The Price of Salt

BY PATRICIA HIGHSMITH

PATRICIA HIGHSMITH

AMERICAN NOVELIST

- **Born in Fort Worth in 1921.**
- **Died in Locarno in 1995.**
- **Notable works:**
  - *Strangers on a Train* (1950), novel
  - *The Talented Mr. Ripley* (1955), novel
  - *A Dog's Ransom* (1972), novel

Patricia Highsmith was one of the most important thriller and mystery writers of the 20th century. Her work explores the psychological underpinnings behind criminal minds and investigates the philosophical questions behind crime, including the notions of good and evil.

A number of her novels explore the personalities of criminals and seek to uncover how a person can deviate far enough from social norms to become a murderer.

Highsmith wrote 22 novels and several short story collections and essays, and her works have been adapted numerous times for the cinema and the theatre. She first rose to fame after Alfred Hitchcock (1899-1980) adapted her novel *Strangers on a Train* in 1951, and her career spanned five decades. One of her most important works is the Ripley series, commonly known as the "Ripliad", which started with *The Talented Mr. Ripley* and follows the life of a charming con artist and serial killer.

In her personal life, Highsmith was known for her hostile manners and reclusive character. Throughout her life, Highsmith had alcohol abuse problems and suffered from cyclical depression, as well as a number of other physical and mental conditions.

THE PRICE OF SALT

LOVE WITH A HAPPY ENDING

- **Genre:** novel
- **Reference edition:** Highsmith, P. (1984) *The Price of Salt*. Tallahassee: Naiad Press.
- **1ˢᵗ edition:** 1952
- **Themes:** love, chance encounters, LGBT rights, romantic relationships, coming of age

The Price of Salt was Patricia Highsmith's second novel. It explores how two very different women (a rich, unhappily married blonde and a solitary 19-year-old bohemian) fall in love in New York in the 1950s, and the obstacles they must face.

Highsmith was inspired to write the novel by her own experience: when she was working as a sales clerk at a department store, she became infatuated with a client, a wealthy, much older woman wearing a fur coat who asked for a doll. Based on that encounter and later that night, in a feverish state, Highsmith wrote most of the plot for the book.

Although upon its first publication as a hardcover, the novel received mixed reviews, it became extremely popular in its paperback version. Hundreds of thousands of readers became interested in a fictional love story between two women that ended well, an extremely rare case.

Initially, Highsmith published *The Price of Salt* under the pseudonym of Claire Morgan. In the 1989 afterword to the reissue (published as *Carol* under Highsmith's own name), Highsmith explained that she did so out of fear of being labelled a lesbian fiction writer, just like she had been labelled a mystery and crime writer after the publication of *Strangers on a Train*.

SUMMARY

AN ENCOUNTER THAT CHANGES EVERYTHING

Therese Belivet, a 19-year-old girl, works at a department store called Frankenberg's, waiting for her first work experience related to her true passion: theatre set design. She leads a solitary life (as her father died and her mother abandoned her), and her only companion is her boyfriend Richard. However, she is not particularly in love with him or excited to spend her future with him.

One day, an elegant fur coat-wearing woman called Carol buys a suitcase at Therese's counter and then comes back for a doll, leaving her address for the delivery. Therese feels strangely attracted to this woman and decides to send her a Christmas card.

Carol calls her at Frankenberg's, amused and intrigued by Therese's card, and invites her to have lunch with her. During lunch, Carol shows an interest in knowing about Therese's life and invites her to visit her home on Sunday.

Therese feels ecstatic about having met Carol, although she is unsure of calling these feelings love, as she has never heard of such a thing happening between women. They meet again at Carol's home and get closer, but their day is interrupted when Carol's soon-to-be ex-husband, Harge, comes home to pick up some things for Rindy, their daughter. He does not like Therese being in the house, and Therese decides to leave.

AN UNNAMED FEELING GROWS

The next day, Carol picks up Therese at Frankenberg's and explains that she and Harge are divorcing. Later, they spend the day together buying a Christmas tree and, as it gets late, Therese stays the night in the guest room.

The next morning, Abby, a friend of Carol's, comes to visit Carol at home. Therese realises that they have a very close relationship and feels slightly envious. Abby suggests that Carol should go on a trip to forget about her divorce issues.

While spending Christmas with Richard and his family, Therese realises that she does not love Richard, but she does loves Carol instead. She also gets her first job for a few weeks as a set designer.

Carol invites Therese to go on the trip with her and Therese agrees, especially after Carol opens up to her about how Harge wanted to control her during their marriage and how their marriage ended.

When Carol gives her a cheque for the trip's expenses, Therese refuses to accept it and leaves it in Carol's guest room. By mistake, she also leaves a secret letter she has written to Carol, where she explains her romantic feelings for her. Before the trip, Therese breaks up with Richard, who is very bothered by this.

THE ROAD TRIP: AN ESCAPE AND A SINCERE LOVE

Carol and Therese go on a road trip with no clear destination. During the first days of their trip, they grow closer and feel freer to tell each other details about their past life.

One day, Therese notices that Carol is carrying a revolver in her suitcase. Carol says that it is Harge's and that she hopes she will not need to use it.

When they arrive in Chicago and drink to celebrate how happy they feel about their trip, Therese thinks of asking Carol to sleep with her, but she does not in the end. The next night, they both tell each other their feelings and they sleep together.

When Therese tries to touch Carol's arm in public the next day, Carol warns her not to, and explains that she does not want to repeat what happened with Abby. She explains that they had a romantic relationship in the past which did not end well because Harge discovered it.

LOVE AT RISK

A telegram from Abby arrives, warning them that Harge has hired a detective to follow them, in order to accuse Carol of indecent behaviour to try to keep Rindy away from her. They feel terrified, but refuse to give up and try to lose the detective.

In their hotel room in Denver, they find a microphone, and later on the highway, they make the detective stop his car. Carol considers shooting him, but pays him for the recorded tapes, even though he says that he has already sent most of them to New York.

After calling Abby, they decide that Carol will fly to New York while Therese will stay on the road with Carol's car, waiting for Carol to deal with her situation. In New York, Carol learns that Harge has found Therese's love letter hidden in the guest room, which will be used against Carol during the trial.

CAROL SURRENDERS AND THERESE IS TRANSFORMED

Carol sends a letter to Therese telling her that she decided to surrender at the trial: the judges consider their relationship immoral, and they made her promise that, if she wants to see her daughter a few weeks a year, she must never see Therese again.

Therese feels betrayed by Carol and becomes depressed. However, one day, she starts feeling better: she realises that she is young and talented and starts looking forward to building a new, more mature and confident life. When Abby calls her and tells her that Carol wants to hear from her, Therese initially refuses to contact her, but ends up accepting to meet Carol to give her back the car.

Carol and Therese meet for tea and Carol says that, at the trial, she finally refused to promise to never see Therese again. As a consequence, she cannot see Rindy for now. Carol adds that she has bought an apartment and asks Therese to move in with her, but Therese declines her invitation, fearing that Carol might break her heart again. They finish their date, as Carol must meet some people at another restaurant and Therese is going to a party.

At the party, Therese meets an attractive young actress who seems very interested her, but Therese realises she will never feel the same way about anyone as she does about Carol. Therese goes to meet Carol at the restaurant and tell her that she wants to spend the future with her. She arrives at the dining hall, both women's eyes meet across the room and they smile at each other.

CHARACTER STUDY

THERESE BELIVET

Therese Belivet is a solitary 19-year-old girl whose relationship with Carol makes her evolve from a timid, indecisive teenager to a resolute and driven adult.

Therese's father died when she was younger and her mother practically abandoned her when she was 14 at a boarding school run by nuns. She has grown up being solitary, and before meeting Carol her social relationships are scarce: her boyfriend Richard is almost the only one she can count on.

However, she is not emotionally invested in her relationship with Richard. She does not think she is in love with him, and is not excited about making any plans with him, like travelling to Europe. When Carol asks her why she is in a relationship with Richard, Therese mentions him being nice and having a family, in which Therese feels safe.

She is extremely introverted and, although many thoughts are in her head, she often finds it difficult to voice them. For instance, although she is practically disengaged from her relationship with Richard, she does not dare to end it. The same happens with Carol, to the point where Carol often asks her what is going on in her mind.

When she meets Carol, Therese's life and personality are completely transformed. Slowly, she is able to recognise her feelings for Carol and let them grow into a relationship, with responsibilities and true commitment.

This relationship takes Therese on an emotional rollercoaster: first, she becomes completely infatuated with Carol. When they confirm their mutual feelings, Therese feels ecstatic. Then, during the detective's persecution and the break-up, her anxiety grows and turns into desolation, but she manages to become empowered by what has happened with Carol. Finally, only after having been through everything, she is able to start living with Carol on an equal basis. She is less dependent and more confident about herself and her abilities.

Her career also transforms thanks to her relationship with Carol. At the beginning of the book, Therese works at a department store but feels constrained by this as her real ambition is to work as a set designer in the theatre. Career-wise, it is only through other people's determination that she is able to land her first job. She is anxious about the future and about becoming who she wants to be, but feels too scared to start it herself. Through Carol's reassurance and her adventurous affair, she is able to find her own opportunities by the end of the book.

Her transformation into empowerment is also visible. After overcoming her break-up with Carol, Therese decides to spend money on buying elegant clothes and changing her hair. This is noticed by many characters, including Carol, who mention how they almost could not recognise her by the end of the book.

CAROL AIRD

Carol is a woman in her thirties from an affluent background whose life is also completely turned around by her meeting with Therese.

Everything the readers learn about Carol is from Therese's point of view, thus revealing her personality as Therese discovers it. In fact, many of Carol's thoughts are revealed by her outside actions. For instance, readers can notice she is anxious when she suggests having a drink or starts smoking cigarettes.

Carol's features (tall, blonde and blue-eyed, with a serene voice and always impeccably dressed) make her an extremely attractive woman who is easily noticed when in public.

She is fiercely independent in a world where women of her position are expected to be compliant and stay at home. This is visible when, during her trip with Therese, she explains how her opening a furniture store with Abby made Harge and his family angry.

In fact, even though by the end of their marriage they had grown bored of each other, her divorce from Harge becomes difficult and vengeful mainly because of Carol's independence. As Carol explains, when Harge married her, he saw her as an object to possess rather than a real woman. When Carol embarked on a relationship with

Abby, Harge felt that his pride was threatened, and the same happens when she meets Therese.

She is not afraid of coming across as a confident woman, but is reluctant to show her vulnerabilities. For her, the divorce from Harge is an extremely painful situation, mostly because it involves her daughter Rindy. Carol does not lean on Therese for support at the beginning, and hardly discusses her divorce with Therese. This is because she believes it is her responsibility to deal with it, and because she thinks Therese is too young to know or to carry that weight. As the novel unfolds, and especially after the trip she goes on with Therese, she is more able to show herself to Therese.

Carol is hesitant as to whether to commit to loving Therese or not. Her reasons mainly have to do with past experience: when she got into a relationship with Abby, she realised that having a relationship with a woman involved being confronted with the world, as they would not accept a homosexual relationship. However, she also hesitates about the relationship because of Therese's youth and lack of experience. She believes this relationship could harm Therese's future, as lesbian relationships are not well regarded in society, and thus is reluctant to cause her distress. Finally, Carol is also reluctant because a relationship with Therese will mean she will not be able to keep in touch with Rindy after the divorce.

Carol's confidence is slowly eroded by outside factors, mainly by the detective who follows them during the trip, and Harge's harsh divorce terms.

By the end of the book, she regains her strength and pride. In fact, during the trial, she refuses to promise that she will never be romantically involved with Therese. To her, it is clear that the male judges are angry at the fact that an attractive woman is not within any men's reach.

ANALYSIS

A STORY BASED ON HIGHSMITH'S OWN EXPERIENCE

Highsmith explained in the afterword of the 1989 reissue of the novel that she was inspired to write this book by her own experience.

By the end of 1948, with her career as a writer not having bloomed yet, she took a job at a department store, just like Therese does in the book. She had just finished writing *Strangers on a Train* and, waiting for it to be published, she needed to earn some extra money.

Highsmith explains that, one day, a blonde older woman came into the store and bought a doll at her counter, and that she immediately fell in love with her. The woman was wearing a fur coat, just like Carol does in the novel.

That night, Highsmith wrote the plot for the novel in around two hours. She woke up the next day with chicken pox. According to Highsmith, this illness and the fever that came with it probably helped her imagine the plot of *The Price of Salt*.

Her own experiences as a (yet) unfulfilled writer who was coming of age are reflected in Therese's character in *The Price of Salt*.

A STEP FORWARD FOR LESBIAN PULP FICTION

Pulp fiction novels were paperback novellas published in America from the beginning of the 20th century. These fiction works were inexpensive and thus extremely popular, with titles that reached millions of people. Their themes included cowboy stories, crime, drugs and gangsters, and they were usually sold in drug stores or train or bus stations.

At the time *The Price of Salt* was published, there had been a number of other pulp novels written about two women falling in love. These included *Women's Barracks* by Tereska Torrès (published in 1950), and *Spring Fire,* written by Marijane Meaker under the pseudonym of Vin Packer (written in 1952). Both novels sold more than a million copies.

Both these books and others which are similar are labelled lesbian pulp fiction. What most had in common is that, as stated by many authors years later, the editors forced the writers to make the characters either die at the end or be admitted to a mental institution. Lesbian relationships were often called "forbidden relationships", and the publishers' goal was to avoid representing homosexuality as a positive thing, in order to overcome censorship.

This is referenced by Carol in *The Price of Salt,* as she speaks of having heard that some girls like girls, but adds that books always said this never ended well, and that it was something that goes away with age.

The Price of Salt became the first novel to portray two women falling in love and having a happy ending. Furthermore, as opposed to the most popular lesbian pulp fiction novels, *The Price of Salt* presented its characters as mentally sound.

After being reissued as a paperback, the novel became a huge success, picking up where the rest of the lesbian pulp fiction novels had left off. From there, more uplifting endings became possible.

As Highsmith explains in the afterword printed in novel's reissue in 1989, the novel was welcome by a great number of people who saw themselves represented by the plot and appreciated how these love stories did not always have to have a tragic ending. Highsmith describes how, after the novel's publication, she received dozens of letters every day (addressed to Claire Morgan, her pseudonym) thanking her for having written the book and even asking for advice. Highsmith added that she was happy to have published a book that supported and helped some people who were leading solitary lives.

COMING OF AGE

The Price of Salt is constructed around Therese's coming of age and how this change shapes her relationship with Carol.

Therese goes through a major transformation during the novel. At the beginning of the book, she lacks confidence and is unable to voice her own preferences. She also finds it difficult to pursue her own career goals, and only advances towards them when pushed to do so by Richard or Richard's acquaintances. Romantically, she is not invested in her relationship and does not seem interested in being sexually involved with Richard or making any plans with him for the future. She seems to be drifting through life rather than finding her own path and becoming herself.

Her meeting with Carol takes her out of her comfort zone and completely transforms her personality. At the beginning, however, their relationship is unequal. On the one hand, Carol is a strong, independent and mature woman who has always found the drive to live life the way she wants. On the other hand, Therese is just beginning to realise what she wants and what she needs in order to be fulfilled. This imbalance continues to the point where Carol breaks up with Therese via a long letter.

This leaves Therese heartbroken and alone again. However, during the days she spends alone waiting to return to New York after the road trip, Therese undergoes a major transformation, which is also visible from the outside. She buys new clothes, gets a new haircut and starts wearing lipstick. On the other hand, she refuses to see or write to Carol, even though Abby asks her to.

By the end of the book, Therese has become a grown adult who knows what she wants and goes for it. This can be seen in her last encounter with Carol. By this point, Carol has become more vulnerable (her divorce has failed and she is not allowed to see her child), and she is the one who asks Therese to move into her new apartment with her. Although at first Therese refuses the offer (afraid of giving the power back to Carol, and thus becoming vulnerable to a potential new break-up), she ends up accepting. However, she has now become an adult and a much more powerful individual.

A LOVE STORY

The Price of Salt is mainly a love story which portrays falling in love from the point of view of someone who is falling in love for the first time (in this case, Therese).

Therese finds it hard to verbalise her feelings, both because it is the first time she has fallen in love, and because she has fallen in love with a woman. Her love is nonetheless extremely potent, as can be seen in her first trip to Carol's home: when Carol is driving them through an underground tunnel, Therese wishes that the tunnel will collapse on them, covering them so that they will be together forever.

However, their love is deemed inappropriate by society at the time and thus faces a number of obstacles. As Carol warns Therese, most people believe their love is an abomination, and will reject and punish them for being together. Carol is also extremely careful about giving in to their relationship, as she believes this could harm Therese in the future.

The biggest obstacle to their love is the fact that Carol is forced to choose between her daughter and Therese by a court whose only accusation is Carol's sexuality. However, Carol overcomes this interference and, as the independent woman she is, refuses to surrender to what the court wants her to do, as this will go against her own personality.

FURTHER REFLECTION

SOME QUESTIONS TO THINK ABOUT...

- Todd Haynes' film adaptation of *The Price of Salt* changed many elements of the plot. List the differences and discuss whether these changes add to the plot or not.
- Abby's character is much more present in the book than in Todd Haynes' film adaptation. Reflect on how this character helps Carol and Therese evolve in their relationship.
- Consider how Carol is known by the readers only through Therese's view of her, and how Carol's character is created by revealing her personality and secrets little by little. What are the effects of this approach?
- Discuss the novel's comments about the persecution of the LGBT community, mainly voiced by Carol after her trial.
- Explore how Therese's personality evolves from immature and insecure to adult, and record the key moments that build this change.

- Carol and Therese's relationship goes through a major shift in power, from Carol being the powerful one to Therese having the future of their relationship in her hands at the end. Mark which moments make this relationship evolve.
- The novel is based on an encounter Highsmith herself experienced with an older woman. Consider whether there are other autobiographical elements, particularly whether Therese's character may be related in some way to a young Highsmith.
- Analyse Harge's character, in terms of how his role as a possessive husband oppresses Carol as a wife, and what this says about Highsmith's ideas of marriage.

We want to hear from you!
Leave a comment on your online library
and share your favourite books on social media!

FURTHER READING

REFERENCE EDITION

- Highsmith, P. (1984) *The Price of Salt*. Tallahassee: Naiad Press.

REFERENCE STUDIES

- Hart, K. (2011) The Inner Life of Patricia Highsmith. *This Recording*. [Online]. [Accessed 22 November 2018]. Available from: <http://thisrecording.com/today/2011/8/15/in-which-patricia-highsmith-endures-a-depression-equal-to-he.html>
- Smith, N. (2015) When Patricia Highsmith Offered Gay Readers a Hopeful Ending. *The New Republic*. [Online]. [Accessed 22 November 2018]. Available from: <https://newrepublic.com/article/124220/patricia-highsmith-offered-gay-readers-hope-ful-ending>

ADDITIONAL SOURCES

- Highsmith, P. (2001) *Plotting and Writing Suspense Fiction*. London: St. Martins Griffin.
- Wilson, A. (2010) *Beautiful Shadow: A Life of Patricia Highsmith*. London: Bloomsbury.

ADAPTATIONS

- *Carol.* (2015) [Film]. Todd Haynes. Dir. USA: The Weinstein Company.

MORE FROM BRIGHTSUMMARIES.COM

- Reading guide – *Strangers on a Train* by Patricia Highsmith.
- Reading guide – *The Talented Mr Ripley* by Patricia Highsmith.

www.brightsummaries.com

Ebook EAN: 9782808016292

Paperback EAN: 9782808016308

Legal Deposit: D/2018/12603/575

Cover: © Primento

Digital conception by Primento, the digital partner of
publishers.